The Blue Island

The Blue Island

Poems by

Douglas Cole

Cover art "Eisberg Im Nibel," by Gerhard Richter
Cover design by Shay Culligan

ISBN: 978-1-949229-26-4

Kelsay Books
Aldrich Press
www.kelsaybooks.com

Other Books by Douglas Cole

The Gold Tooth in the Crooked Smile of God (Poetry)
Bali Poems (Poetry)
The Dice Throwers (Poetry)
Western Dream (Poetry)
Interstate (Poetry)
Ghost (Novella)

Acknowledgments

I gratefully acknowledge the journals in which the following poems appeared:

"Off Season Travelers," *Ascent*
"The Wolf" (from "Oblivion Night"), *The Atlanta Review*
"Penrose Staircase," *Bindweed Anthology: Devil's Guts*
"Five Points Bar and Grille," "The Cave," "The Eye Opens" (from "Oblivion Night"), *Black Heart Magazine*
"Travelers," *Bleeding Typewriter*
"Siren Song," *Crossways, Coe Review*
"Winterfalling," "Eat Stone and Go On," *Degenerate Literature*
"Ascent," *Eclectica*
"The Bog," "Double Bluff," *The Galway Review*
"The Endless Roads," "Elysian Fields," *Gray Sparrow Press*
"Slipping Through the Zones," *Genre: Urban Arts*
"Eat Stone and Go On," *HCE Review*
"Off Season Travelers," *The Heartland Review*
"On Entering," *Hobo Camp*
"The Star," *Inklette Magazine*
"Catch and Release," *Longleaf Review*
"Thank the Wind Alive," *Mojave River Review*
"Diamond," "What Should I Say," *The Pangolin Review*
"Doghouse," *Picaroon Poetry Journal*
"Fast Awake," *Rogue Agent Journal*
"Outcast," *Stoneboat*
"Thought Experiment," "Morphic Field Hotel," "The Kiss of Life," *Synchronized Chaos*
"Theme," *Two Thirds North*
"Tullianum," *The Tower Journal*
"Elysian Fields," *Visions*
"At the Silver Tray Bar," *Visions International*
"Penrose Staircase," *Woven Tale Press*

Contents

Island Time

Ascent to the Gallows

Theme

Late night maybe morning
          heading home through
          wet dark streets
under the glow of
          fleur-de-lis lanterns
          with their minaret globes
she climbs the stairs
          the carpeted smell of years
to enter a room overlooking
          the gray slate rooftops
          and redbrick chimneys
          and that one lone tower
          under the blood smear of clouds
          in a smoky predawn haze
to fall back upon a bed
          after the search that yielded
          nothing now but this now
hearing the crazy neighbors
          and other voices
          and one sound like
a trumpet call
          like a wish for death
          and sweet release through
          the bottom of the well
          of elusive sleep
with a ghost at the door
          and water traveling through
          the pipes in the wall

The Assassination

Where are you
where'd you go
the street is
loaded with ghosts
and the worker rises
puts on coat and gloves
and plunges into the cold
out with the streetlamps
cry out the news
lift your hands and feel
the faint
warmth of the sun

The Endless Roads

Awake and go
       stomping down
       to the crowded street
grab a café au lait
       and a day-old croissant
head out into the cold air
       hustle and bustle of human
       faces faces everywhere
take the stairs to the bridge
       to the upper hill road
       stacked up white stone buildings
       with bleak green awnings
       and dark windows full of smoke
looking for the address
       of the old actress in her mansion tomb
       with her kept man
       clutching his diamond tie pin
       and Bentley phone
floating face down to earth
       close up on the worms
       doing their work

Ascent

It's so quiet
       you can hear a heartbeat
in the distance
       a sound
       a siren
       a whistle or a bell
the wood walls
the gray windows looking out
       onto street level
       feet passing
       tires hissing
time ticking
       on a grandfather clock
trio on the bandstand
       a bass player
       piano player
trumpet player smoking
       his eyes full of gage

Elysian Fields

You enter the Zen garden
with a blue pool steaming
the mist rising through
the limbs of a red-leaf maple
rocks shape-shifting
from an old man gazing
through his monocle
to an old owl flying free
from a stone peak
the hand of the artist
now touching
the end of a fern leaf
bowed with one clear
drop of rain
and yellow grass
like eyelashes
draped over a waterfall
and then you look up
and see
framed by the fence
the rooftop and the trees
waves of geese
passing like a dream

Travelers

Train station
train arriving
steam smoke rising
and surrounding the engine
people descending
travelers diving
into the city
with wide eyes of wonder
and carnival desires
to fill their pockets with
ticket stubs and tokens
timetables and theater bills
while new passengers boarding
take their seats
and place their faces
in the window frames
to look out at you
and the big train moves back
heading down the black
parallel tracks
into forever fields
green rolling and flush
with tan bare trees at the edge
and silo dome farm houses
embedded there among empty
plowed rows
under a sky stroked
with fire and blood

Escape

No class
no poverty
no homelessness
'less you want it
make your music
make your way
go roll your bones
and sing your praises
well and true

A Visit from the Guard

He was a real cool cat
        that artist
        that dude
he made climbing into a cab
        look like a dance move
and with a flourish of the gods
        the night for him is
        a smorgasbord of possibilities
cocktails with the princess
        a show at the Met
        a trip to the spa
        for a massage and a soak
        in the blue jet pool
        glowing in the rooftop garden
and nearby at hand a helipad
        a chariot with silent rotors
        lifting us over
        skyscraper pinpoints
        and city street arteries
the world is your oyster
        crack it open
valets guide you
        to your next engagement
touch and counter touch
        smile and smile
        have a drink
        relax by the fire
nothing but everything
        at your whim
        for a while

At The Silver Tray Bar

Meeting with the producer
  we disagree on the ending
who'll play the lead
  and the ingénue
will it be a chance meeting in Rome
  or Venice and then
  Greek Isles for the rendezvous
complications of war
  with a sex scene interlude
juxtapose kissing and love smiles
  with V after V of
  passing warplanes
and a soundtrack mixed
  with hope and despair
and let's get that photographer from Paris
  to shoot the stills
  the one who caught
  the assassination of Jacques
  and did Jane on the cover of *Life*
we'll work on post-production in Nice
  and maybe have
  the wrap party there
set that Jew on distribution
  he's got the connections
then work out the markets
  the tour for promotions
and even get that gypsy girl
  who worked on *Mundo*
  and found those victims
  through remote viewing
she'll help us out
  with a little prayer

Photographer of the Dead

I should be home by Christmas
  a few details left
  to work out
a few palms to grease
  and I'll be glad
to kick free of this place
  these slick charmers
gendarmes smoking cigarettes
  bad food in a country
  that invented cuisine
time like a teardrop
  window in the storm
and I recall now
  a gavel sound
  a trap door and a fall
or was it a dream
  a wave in the sea of sleep
I don't know
  I don't care to know
now that I am at last free
  more free than I've ever been
and I see like Hubble's telescope
  looking into deepest space
your face my love
  and the black hole
  at the center of your eye

Oblivion Night

"Courage," he said, and pointed toward land,
"This mountain wave will roll us shoreward soon."
—Alfred Lord Tennyson
The Lotus Eaters

In a still sky
fretted with golden fire
one black bird soars,
the most beautiful melody,
and so the day begins…

This is where I had a drink
with a friend in a Left Bank café,
windows full of steam,
and we talked about school days,
travel, art, America at the end
and the beginning,
then out to the cinema,
club boulevard overflowing
with rock and roll circus
hucksters and booze hounds,
and with a few bundles of wood
under each arm, I climbed the stairs
to a rented room and there,
alone, in an amniotic sea bath,
I slipped away….

When I was on a three-day bender,
four if you count Thursday night,
the only conscious thing I did
was shower and shave,
somewhere, somehow, each day—
come out of the fog for a bit,
get my bearings, try for morning,
wherever I was, wherever I ended up.
Otherwise, there was no real program—
rise early, gut full of razors,
smoke and try for an appetite,
but if that didn't work,

go straight for the beer
and a few shots of whiskey—
anything to even out—
use no magic other than
medicine pouch and prayer,
then tumble through the red door
into the dark of Dante's Bar,
dirty room floating like a
Dianna Camera photograph,
faces blurry at the edges,
bartender woman chopping
limes and fingers,
scanning with sinister glare
and baring her iron teeth,
friends, friends all around,
the air full of smoke trails,
eyes blotted by conjunctivitis,
blood under the bathroom door,
and she's wiping her lips
as the darts fly, points glistening,
feather tails hissing
right into the corkboard,
hitting with a bullet sound—
and through blown-out rubble-brick
sidewall see the comedian arrive,
tumbling out of a slipstream trailer
silver gleaming in the street,
accompanied by rhinestone assistants
in jumpsuits and star sunglasses
and fluttering ostrich feather wings,
who fall into this under-freeway
hovel among the slouching
droolers and slack-jaw pool players
and red-light silk-skin
entertainers leaning in doorways…

Lost in the trumpet vine court
night pathways to everywhere,

among blue-lit bungalows
under morning glory flowers,
ghosts crowd the archways.
What a new miracle!
And then the bugle call,
and I recall the message—
I'm a conduit to some idea.

How the marionettes dance.
I follow strangers.
The janitor shuffles
with the gait of the afflicted,
hands twitching,
and I wonder if inside
he sees with clarity
these people watching
with mixed emotions of
sympathy fear disgust
as he swings his loose-held head
and dim, half-open eyes.

Cops hassle a kid
on the corner of 3rd and Pike,
as three old women,
bent and palsied,
trundle loud-talking
and take their seats
in the theater
to watch a cartoon.
Information for the witness stand,
details for an alibi.

Let the adventures begin
when dawn light hits
like a storm of Jehovah's Witness
pamphlets sweeping down
workers on Western Avenue.
Who's got the rot-gut

and nowhere to go?
I got what I asked for,
oh ye gods,
and you know how to deliver
every wish, every prayer
in some variation,
knowledge and a little punishment—
there on the burning beach,
a flyer floating up onto my foot,
and I reach down and read it:
Missing Person!
Along with a photograph.
And there find another
tacked on a wall.
Some guy's gone missing.
He was last seen in Duke's
on Christmas Eve,
and I wonder,
was it a fight,
a murder,
or did he just disappear
from his life,
deciding one day
I'm through and walking
right out of it.

Woman,
I inherited your nightmares.
We're not talking about love, here,
we're talking about soul
and psychic empathic transfer.
I get a call from an old friend
who says he's getting married,
and I say,
do people still do that?
He isn't amused.
And it seems like I've gotten
more tickets than usual this year.

At a certain age the child sees
that the parents are just
part of the landscape,
that their decisions
and their "influences" are
as much a part of the empty lot,
the trappers shack, the rain,
and the steaming, stinky coats
in the elementary school closet,
moving, moving and break-up—
smaller and smaller rooms…
homelessness and winter storm,
sickness and slow recovery,
and then we're left
to decide how to tell it all.
We come to a promontory
at various points
from which to view the road…
that's the moment, my friends,
when everything becomes
most uncertain and clear.

I use the theater
as a place to duck away
when I'm lost or high
or too drunk to drive
or otherwise can't go home.
Doesn't matter what's showing
or what the weather is like
or what time of day.
I float on into the dark
dreamhouse with its carpet walls
and sticky cement floors
and plush rocking chairs
where I settle into the shadows…
sometimes I see something good,
sometimes I pass right out
and sink through the floor...

later I wake freshly bewildered
and ready to re-enter the world…

I was in character,
reaching like a toreador for the holy water
when we passed through the doors
of Saint Mark's Cathedral
for Sunday night vespers.
And I was feeling like Sean Penn
in *Hurly Burly* when
someone tried to hand him a baby.
Believing what they believe,
which is to remember my father,
my sons, the cloth of creation,
the deep codes of what I am,
patterns discovered and broken
and recreated like rewritten prayers,
so I think about every move,
the empty alley after midnight,
and passing it all down,
and how do you reconcile that?
Or even understand the butterflies,
the ramifications?
Had I done this—
Had I done that—
Where's my hat?
and effects that keep on happening.
Sons, most specifically,
know in a moment like this
I think of you in my twilight,
in all my border wanderings,
with my most acute awareness,
that with or without you,
I am in your presence
in my best self with nothing
but blessings and love to offer
forever and ever…

Coming out on the other side
of Truth and Divine
under a halo of wisteria vines,
heading down the steps to the docks
and Mark's houseboat there
listing in its berth,
bathed in music and sunlight,
I enter the dark front cabin,
pass through the galley kitchen,
dishes piled in the sink,
duck through the low-ceiling living room
and come out onto the deck
with its red pots full of sunflowers
and poppies with their dusky eyes,
as Charlie tosses me a can of beer
from a plastic cooler filled with ice,
and he's grinning mushroom clouds
green gold around his head,
says, "so listen, that madman
friend of Ed's comes over for a barbecue,
and Mike hands him a plate with a steak,
but he's only got one arm, right,
so he just looks up and says, 'what
the fuck am I supposed to do with this?'
He asks me for notes on his script
ah…he doesn't know what he's doing,
but it's not that bad, you know,
and this isn't the first chance I've taken,
so I just said, 'I'm in it for the money…'"
Life becomes more glamorous in telling,
and the Florida woman dreams
in her room overlooking the sea
under the same sun sliding through
an electric kaleidoscope sky
like a hot dime blazing in a pool…
and the sunglory hillside burns
with roots and tendrils shimmering,
conscious and humming alive,

water slap-tapping the edge of the dock,
rolling rippling and smoothing out,
as dandelions dance and explode
like liquid diamond shards of fire…
O majesty O sunlight O source,
O blazing crown of heaven…
everything is made from laughter,
and tomorrow's children emerge
with machinegun hearts
in their Mahayana chests,
sparks in the void
and the house of our knowing…

And this same light,
this same violet sky
spreads over Puerto Vallarta
cliff divers hitting with pinpoint
entry the white waves below,
re-emerging moments later
bursting from the surface,
and we set up our little bar on deck,
with margaritas and Tecate
on the lost weekend vogue terrace
with movie star magazines
and bodies and looks of glamour,
no hardware or money but
catching the buzz just the same,
as the sun egg-flattens on the sea,
shimmering
gone…

When you're on a three-day bender
there inevitably comes
a moment when you slip,
when the chemical levels dip,
and you catch a glimpse of yourself,
in a bathroom with green tile
and overflowing trash

and the darkest rank odor
of cloacal human existence,
and there in the mottled mirror
you see not what
you would recognize as yourself
but an amplified monster mask,
eyes glowing like two dull coals
embedded in wet cement,
and the urge to look further is
only overridden by
the need to vomit,
and then you're on your way
believing it was all a dream.

Then there's the woman of the rocks.
She's known by many names:
red-haired ticket-taker at the turnstile
with a narrow elevator smile,
blond screamer in the red mustang,
the wild-eyed, snake-haired goddess
who stares you into stone,
and of course the witches
churning the contents of the cauldron,
stirring the sky blood-boiling red
with whirlwind and fury,
crackling dry laughter
and lightning lighting the city,
lighting the docks and the waves,
with stowaways under the planks
in the ship that arrives for thee…

All play on the beach has ended,
dust rises where sun bathers lay,
glistening beauty on parade,
then dive fights at Pepperdocks
with no idea…sunlight about to go,
shutters closing, engines revving up,
everything returning to the way it was

but never the same, here at a glance
in the last chance lurch of desire…
the sidewalk rolling its conveyor belt,
the moon throwing its rope ladder down,
cops scanning the driftwood with flood lights,
and shadow by shadow we roll and stroll
until we flow right out of it.

This is where Dennis Hopper died,
wild man, movie maker, actor, star—
headlines, news on the television,
as I drink Black Label with Tony
in his first floor apartment
that is otherwise dark year-round
except on this one summer day
when light comes like a magic ray
down the walkway and through the door,
with those alley cats eyeballing us
as they slide by feral and mean,
and I'm sure they're waiting to feed
on the first one of us to fall asleep,
while Cowles Mountain burns—
imagine it, a whole mountain on fire
(and it is!) from dry summer tinder
white lightning days—
Tony leaning over sea charts
and a San Juan Islands guide book,
stories of deep water passages
and drifting cabin wave sleep,
glowing spring sunlit mornings
diving into the waters of the Sound,
and it all sounds so perfect,
so idyllic as this cat sits there
watching me with narrow,
I'll-outlast-you eyes.
Get lost, you demon! Go, now!
Payment isn't due, yet!
And I feel my whole act slipping.

It was dangerous lunacy,
but it was also the kind of thing
a real connoisseur of edgework
could make an argument for.
You were a schemer, you had plans,
and look what that got you!
This is what happens when
an unstoppable force
meets an immovable object.

Gravity Attack
Man Down

It's the lulls that kill ya.
The depressions in the landscape
where one makes fatal decisions,
or worse, suffers indecision,
in the gap in the pause
in the brutal hesitation—
as the bus comes barreling down
the wrong side of the street
(wrong to me since
I'm out of my element),
because I'm looking the other way,
and it's just a nudge of instinct
that brings me around,
and I feel that rush of wind
at my back and see that look
on your face and realize
my head was leaning into that—
it could have gone a different way—
when you're in that slipstream,
that fateful hollow glow.

Awake!
With Boy-F-Doggie,
failed army grunt,
standing over my bed,

staring down,
sneering down,
pointing at the ground and saying,
"You look as empty as that bottle."

Say nothing, make no mistake.
All energy flows
according to the great magnate.
From destitution in a motel bed,
to inspection by a park ranger
while my girlfriend gives me head
in the meadow next to the trail,
to blackout in the bathroom stall—
fighting for survival in the bible hall,
love crawling from the muck of the lake
and quick convulsions that palliate
the clap of thunder in the squall.
We gravitate according to the great magnate.
I understand this now.

Dark Bar, haven or hell…
the pretty waitress floating around
and the bartender flirting, saying,
Ladies and gentlemen, boys and girls—
I present you Miss America!
Now, what was it like growing up
in that pageant system?
Applause? Laughter…
All's right with the world, or is it?
See here? See this bad vein
all black and bunched up?
That's what I got from my Angel love,
my angel of death,
that and this black eye
and this compass I steer my ship by
and always back to her.
She summoned me out of the desert.
It's true. In a ceremony.

She wrote me right into her life.
How do you deny that kind of power?
That kind of magic?
And I'm saying this, I think,
looking into the deep
uncomprehending eyes of a turn-key
who only came in to ask for directions.
Pearls before swine! I say,
as he jots down a few notes
on a wet bar napkin.
Pearls before swine!

On the big stake-out,
I hunker down
in the back of my jeep,
gathering energy
for whatever the great snake
has in store for me.
This is part of the work, you see.
You must be nimble-minded and fit.
You never know what's coming, so
you have to keep your wits about you.

Not through a decision I made
out of compassion,
not consciously seeking,
more in the way I've been
stumbling along with tunnel vision,
I find my old friend
in puckered clothes but still
going by the name of Chuck,
three years into atomizing ALS,
Lou Gehrig's disease, his
hands trembling, eyes miles ahead,
each breath an absolute effort of will.
His dark humor burns inside
as we wander the afternoon streets
and wind up at the Pioneer Hotel bar,

and find there a Victorian scale
as old as the city itself.
Step up, he says, and so I do
and the arm that shows the weight
swings madly but never stops,
and he says as if already dead,
It's measuring the weight of your soul…
But I'm the only one drinking, now,
though with every shot I take
I move closer to that gray zone
where I hear him say,
every day, man, I wake up with it,
staring me in the face, my own face—
there's no way out of it.
And he floats on an Empire Couch
in that office off Yesler,
the early evening headlights
strafing through the windows,
no way out of this, man,
I'll go to sleep and not wake up.
And the room fills up
with his dream life drifting like
contents from a drowned man's coat,
all ghostly in the fish tank glow,
like the painting of the chess player
with a silver watch on a chain,
notes for a novel scrawled
on butcher paper tacked to the wall,
loose change, bank receipts…
and a rosary…he says,
how'd that get in here?

Stirring.
Who's that in the doorway?
Just a shade.
Am I dreaming?
Am I waking up?
I try to rise.

Something pins me down.
Shape in the doorway lifts his arm.
I can't move a muscle.
I'm starting to panic.
Why can't I wake up?
Nothing works.
And then, in the blink of an eye,
light comes through the window.

I breathe.
I rise.
All right, I say,
but you're not there.
That's okay.
Sun's coming up.
At last I made it.

Under the stairs
in a basement room
a spirit lurks.
It's a nasty spiteful ugly
spitting spirit,
and I've known it
for a long time
and always get the same
shuddering skin crawling
feeling of revulsion.
One of these days
I'm going to go
past that urge to look away,
face it, walk right into it,
even though my stomach
turns at the thought of it,
and who knows what
will happen after that.
But I know what I have to do,
one of these days.

Five Points Bar and Grille,
somewhere downtown,
with a sign over the door saying
We Cheat Tourists-N-Drunks Since 1929,
a poor woman out front
leaning down unraveling
bandages from her swollen legs,
a tour group cruising by
with gawking faces staring out,
people lined up outside the foodbank,
others sitting around on iron grates,
nowhere to go on a Sunday afternoon,
streets mostly empty under cloud cover,
cars moving slow and dark,
and police arrive and arrest some kid
who's obviously down on his luck,
and isn't that the way it goes?
When you're down,
gravity just seems to hit harder.
This is not a world for the weak.
The script doesn't have much sympathy.
At least that's how I feel today.
And I know what the tour bus people
with their cameras and their pursed
judgmental looks are thinking,
even with their own abuse stories,
sleeping around and lying about it,
taking the money found in a wallet,
drinking to the brink of oblivion or over.
Some people get away with it.
That's all. That's how it goes.
Another public bus just arrived—
as long as we stay in the city,
we can ride all day for free.

You see, in this
witness protection program,
you get a new face,

a new language,
a new race of people
under a double sun,
vehicles like you've never seen
pulling into docking stations
next to maroon lawns,
and we fly out
and mingle in twilight halls
with a million possibilities,
all this after one little dose,
a few rubberneckers,
a new pronouncement,
a short procession.
What a little payoff can do
for a con artist like me
and a weasel like you:
smile and flash
and shoot right through the roof.

When I woke up,
the cops were hustling
a pile of rags to the squad car.
And I wondered,
why him and not me?
No reason.
No way to define it.
It's just luck.

Then I stumble into
an underground cabaret
circus with lit stages
and naked freaks on ropes,
a huge human fish tank
under a glass-covered floor,
people slipping through red
curtains into black booths,
blond appearing in gothic dress,
fishnet stockings and leather boots,

on the arm of a bald vampire,
zeroing in on big beautiful woman
and her bearded man with a cape
as teeth clamp bare shoulders
closed eyes and little sighs
while other vultures descend
and vampire lifts a drink to her lips—
what nightmare have I slipped into,
the room filling with green smoke,
couples en masse on each other
in random entries, open legs,
wild animal devouring—
I've got to get out of here—
claws reaching for me
as I stagger to the door.

The thing about this journey is
you don't know when it ends.
You slip into it as escape.
but when you come up for air,
you find sharks all around you,
and so you dive back in,
until it becomes a bewildering
water-wheel spinning with no exit—
so pass through the looking glass,
through tree limbs and leaves
where light reveals a child
on the other side of the tracks
running on the golden sand
on a summer day
maybe late July or August,
and he dives into the Sound
and rises like a seal
with head wet black and slick
and skin rich tan I was then,
now how strange looking back
through twilight telescope vision.

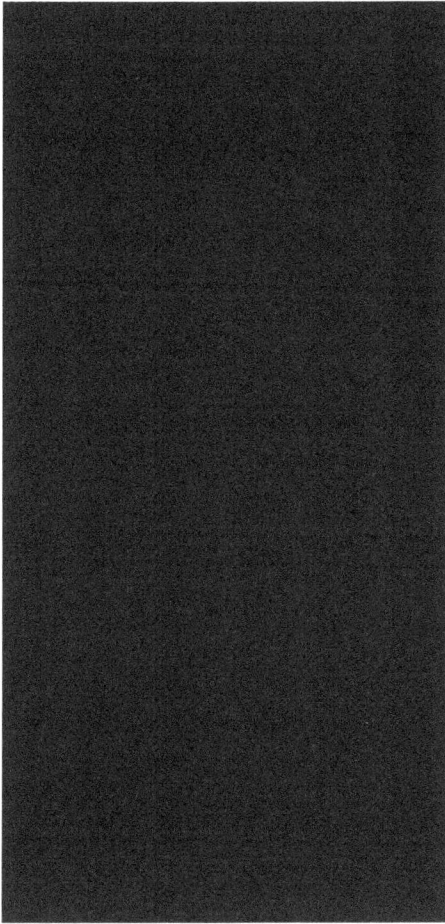

A trip like this sets up
a certain momentum,
gravitational forces take hold,
the ground flowing like snakeskin,
and the rooms spin as people
leer and grin and laughter twists
into something more sinister—
survival mechanisms might kick in
with an urge to get off,
but the vehicle is speeding,
devil at the wheel, no slowing down,
so hang on for the next round

and the one after that.
Stumble beachside
when the flesh people arrive,
the sun fuelers sizzling
like hamburger on the grille,
children digging to China,
Frisbee kids and guitar players
trancing out on the dunes,
gulls squabbling over clams,
dropping crabs like red skydivers
that smash on the rocks…
the horror of meat flesh glistening
and exposed from its shell…
there's no singing or chanting it away,
becoming molecule by molecule
a part of the ground,
my limbs liquid sinking into sand...

And how did I end up here,
in this filthy barbershop,
floor covered with heaps of hair,
getting a haircut from a gay
Vietnamese barber with gray teeth?
Each snip is a loud severance,
blade gleaming near my throat,
hostess biting a fingernail
and a black fly buzzing,
landing and relanding on a mirror,
and I just know
I'll never get out of here alive…

Hauled before the magistrate
I knew this time would come
picked up for passing out
in Lincoln Park
under the shade of a cedar tree,
but for a moment
my eyes were opened,

the light coming through
the branches above,
and I caught a glimpse
of the way
the soul moves
in and out of things—
for a moment
I had it,
but now I have to pay
a big fine,
endure reprimand,
time and more time,
community service,
suspended sentence,
various warnings,
a record,
no vision here,
but I remember…

Of course there were early days
when John Clark and I took
a six pack of Kirin or Dos Equis
up to Tilden park or Lake De Anza
and smoked a bomber,
young and full of dreams
and cynicism and time time time
to design our revenge
on the great monster universe
that plucked us from the deep
celestial drift and threw us into this
jungle, this smog dumpster,
but we saw past the wires
and the cheap lighting
and the oil slick sunset colors
to the pure gold,
as his dog chased down
a deer in the reeds.
And Ronnie gives John and me

a little speed to pep things up
as we drive into San Francisco
and the Hyatt Regency rooftop bar,
spinning so that when I rise
from four or five Harvey Wallbangers,
the tilt-a-whirl room
sends me staggering over thick
velvet floors pitching and rolling,
as I lunge like a pinball
knocked around by some wild
mechanical adolescent gnome,
boom—crash—sorry,
bumping into waitresses,
stumbling into a stranger's chair,
wedding party, bachelorette party,
intimate couple,
and where's my table?
I ask you, who invented this
merry-go-round dining room?
One false step and you're off,
and I can't find my friends,
and there's a human tooth
floating in a martini glass,
slow creatures turning hooded eyes—
wait, it wasn't just speed and rum,
something else slipped in there
under the wire—
what a joke, what a cosmic joke
in the end
as each step sends that foot down there
stretching out seven leagues
seven leagues onward
to land on some checkerboard square,
and any minute now
the great hand is going to pluck me up—
and from far away I hear the call,
the summoning voice, familiar drawl,
Connecticut Yankee and Alabama Belle,

then charming and fair find
smoky arms waving like a pit-crew in hell
as I safely land in the booth
in the spinning night.
Where were you?
Lost!
Lost?
The room is spinning,
my head is spinning,
spinning,
spinning…
oh, who's going to pay the bill?
My hands won't work,
can't see straight,
how are we gonna get out of here?
But we do,
we always do
by the skin of our teeth,
locked in slow descent,
great feathery arms of oblivion—

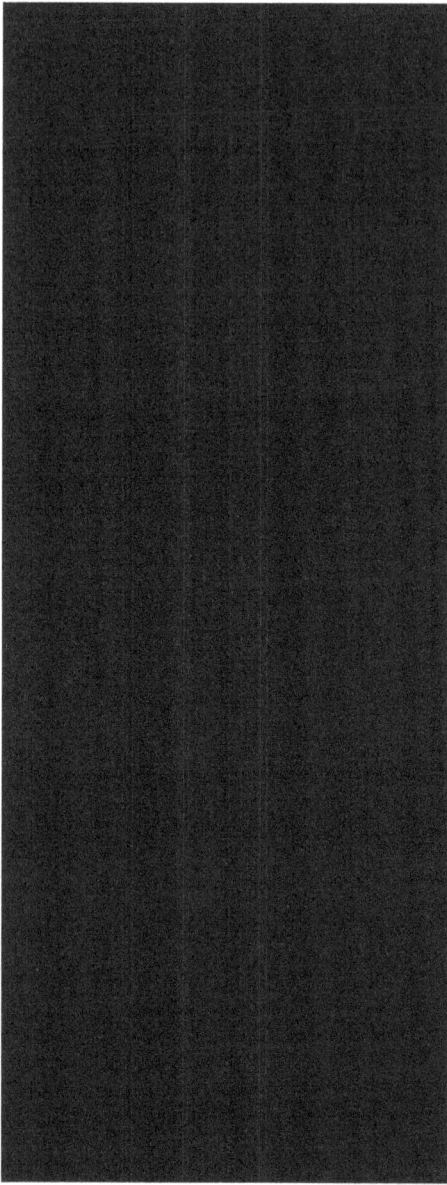

The moon coming up
full and yellow,
a wolf-moon, I think,
meaning somewhere out there
a wolf is roaming

far from the pack,
the way it happens occasionally—
one stops and lifts its head,
scans for something
then trots away,
the others barely glancing
but knowing all the same,
and the one alone sets off
in some direction,
to watch you'd think
there was certainty in that stride,
he knows where he's going,
he chose this course
up over the rise
and into the little box canyon
where his shadow falls
like burnt skin down the slope,
that big moon shining above,
landscape silver with its light,
and that one wolf continues—
maybe he doesn't have a clue,
maybe instinct draws him on—
anything is possible,
I imagine,
with a big yellow moon like that.

A holy woman was my first.
I was fifteen, she was twenty three,
a counselor at the church youth group.
All the boys were crazy for her.
She was picked out by a *Playboy* scout,
offered ten grand to do a photo shoot.
Our thing started one autumn night
as we were walking home together,
fog rolling through live oak trees.
And while leaning in her doorway,
she planted a gentle kiss on me,
a magical soft brush of the lips,

with a halo light around her head,
and then sent me drifting into night.
A beautiful love affair, you might say.
But she was married, did I mention that?
Her husband Tom was a gardener
who didn't pay much attention to her,
while she managed the building,
collected rents and studied nights
to get her teaching certificate.
She hired me to paint apartments,
and we made love in empty rooms.
Her husband eventually figured it out
and told her to end it, simple as that.
I took it like a man, you know?
Walked away, what else could I do?
And that became my stance,
yet that kiss, that divine kiss—
I've been searching for it ever since.

This image of a young man
sitting in the back of a gondola
comes back to me.
I find it flipping through
snapshots of the past, although
I don't have a photographic memory.
But I see him.
He's only twenty one,
but he's got this weary look.
Could be from the traveling.
Could be from sleeping on trains.
Could be from a Munich ghost.
Could be that behind the look
is a realization about love.
Or could be he saw years to come
and so had a knowing that some
lessons are never really learned.
Could be a lot of things.
The only thing I know for sure is

the look on that face never left.
And I know what happens
because I'm here in the future,
like a mirror facing a mirror,
infinite looking back and ahead.

The days are getting shorter,
that's for sure.
And the numbers are adding up.
I keep hoping one day
something will come clear,
something so true in the moment,
a flash of insight
I'll know and won't forget
when another storm comes
or past receipts and wrongs
assert their venom.
Or maybe everything I've read
for years will finally click
and at last express the vision
and my understanding hold.
I keep hoping this as I wonder
what will get me—
these cigarettes?
The thing in my gut?
Or one big wallop to the heart?
I hope for clarity before then,
so I can write it down for you,
and you'll be able to read it
and know it, too.

Jesus in Gethsemane
and later on the hill,
and he said, look at the people,
and I did:
some were horrified,
some were angry,
some were shocked and sad,

others indifferent and bored…
the human face of things…

Wrapped in gauze,
lowered into the crypt,
covered by a stone lid,
sinking in,
drifting,
drifting…

I rise from the dead,
and travel across the desert
in a fast desert wind,
dive into an old form
huddled by a seaside dock,
staring through folds of robes
as siroccos blast the world,
sand obscuring everything,
and all we can do is wait it out…
In the calm after,
I wander the village streets
looking through doorways
at families in their huts
crouching over cooking fires
in rooms lit by oil lamps,
children playing in the dirt…

I conjured the bird,
the black bird,
and it rose like smoke
and coiled above me
with open wings
as I fell into the rich black
open mouth of darkness,
a river of obsidian gold,
tunnels telescoping out
like arteries punching through
spider web rocks to the air above,

and I flowed the open river
into ocean thought and things
floating like shards of glass
under white microscope lights,
worlds enclosed in globes
and books of the ages lined up
on shelves in the Great Library...

Death though humorless
does not inspire terror,
rather a manager's efficiency
and a grim work ethic,
as we ride the soul-loaded ship
out to the margins,
and the periphery of imagining,
where the dead languish
in their indecisive fields,
bent under their long shadows
and far from the meager
light of a distant sun.

And so I go
back through the maze
and the village by the shore,
where I plunge through
pulsing markets
to the cradle of civilization
waiting to explode...

Amazing!
A little pot,
a beer,
and it all seems
so much better.
Maybe I just forget
stuff that doesn't matter,
or maybe I remember
the stuff that does.

Sometime I think I chose
the quiet philosopher's life
puttering in his garden
with god in a dragonfly's eye
as though big life drama
distracts us from the pure
essential
truth and beauty of the world,
then I look back and see
it wouldn't have mattered—
in private,
in poverty,
it all came out the same…
well maybe not exactly
but with the same tax.

I wake and don't remember
the dream I had,
big wind knocking the trees around,
trees banging the side of the house
while I go down on her,
and the wind chimes ring,
and the geese call in passing
as that dream lingers
just out of reach.

The cold that winter
was the worst in memory,
so the locals said.
Snow every step of the way
from my apartment to yours,
and that spooky burned flat,
the story of the murder
and the body found there…
one street lamp shines on the stairs.
It became part of the story of love,
along with steamy crowded pubs,

pints and darts, Toby the omnisexual,
and Leslie writing bad checks
in every country across Europe.
Gray buildings and green dales—
the radiator rattling all night,
papers on Dostoevsky and Proust,
sleep barely come by dawn.
Scratchy sweaters, bangers and beans,
lectures I barely remember…
Venice opens like a flower,
riding down canals in a sad gondola,
then the cruel inn-keeper in Beograd
strangling the cat,
mystery initiation of Crete,
bocce on the beaches of Sweden,
and finally return to the States.
We were kids then, just kids,
what did we know of love's lonely office—

You know, you look back
and you can't always be sure
where things went wrong.
But I tell you, there's a limit
to the number of ways
you can remake your life.
There are only so many
turns you can take.
I've been at this edge
a long time and I've seen
people on the brink,
seen them go over
and no coming back.
Big dreams, big money, love—
take only a moment to destroy.
I've seen people tear it down
for no other reason
than they can.
Stuck in the banishment house,

I watch a cavalcade of strangers
pass through airy rooms, no pity.
Not even much curiosity,
oglers at a train wreck.
When were you last a sober man?
Two? Three years ago?
It isn't so simple, darling.
I waited nights you were away.
I waited… with hope.
How pathetic is that?
And who are these people
who come and go?
I want to drink alone,
die in the arms of love alone
and feel that beautiful agony.

Shy away. Shear back,
for in me you see
the very roots of lechery.
I speak to you in good company,
validated by public decree,
monarchy and noblesse oblige.
From a poisoned failing race
I have one more thing to say:
the greatest threat to intimacy is…glory.
The child of our passion is love, life,
livelihood steeped in escape,
ad caedem igitur vertuntur,
drama, fame, dissipation…
to embrace the world is to embrace
its confusion and calamities,
sickness and passion…for just so long.
So may this last breath be
the moment of liberty.

The Journal of Lord Kensington

Prologue

The fire dancer boys
and the moon-eyed girls
dress their fears in "spirituality"
the beach is bloated with crows
sundowners at the wheel
boats disappearing in darkness
yet here I am offered another day
privilege pain of consciousness
the sparks fly in the void
the slick suit gameshow host
barks at the gate to another ride
I wade through a row of skulls
black holes sucking in with
the rattling promise of a wet kiss

Flight

The moon is a bright jewel eye
looking through the skull of night
down a tunnel that I travel
on my way to dawn light

Dispatch

Now that we have that out of the way
new aviator glasses might be in order
something to hide these alien eyes
cloak this identity because you see
if I were known they'd rip me to pieces
although I can't say I'd miss this
clumsy contraption of limited vision
like being stuck inside a mythology tree
thank the gods from time to time
I escape the machine and all
the intrigues cooked up by the Changer
I love this field beyond the air
you've never seen an ocean
until you've seen these waves

Tullianum

Every moment in this place
I flinch at crows dawn-cawing
and apples falling through leaves
branches scraping the rooftop
as something sleeps beside me
in another fabric of stone
creeping up my fingernails
into this light-deprived skin
walls within walls I live within
and layers of muscle I've trained
by blind hours in solitary motion
in a two foot by two foot room
going nowhere with bones wrapped
by a winter fire built out of need
so what can I tell you about
the glowing walls of mystery
you who can only go so far
restricted as you are by visiting hours
and institutional rules of contact
so I offer a note left after the fact
that says I am here and I am free
and answers for why and how
I can speak quietly into your ear
when you arrive and find nothing
but an empty cell

Hawks Meadow

Can't claw my way out of this haze
rescue planes flying over for days
what could possibly be left
cinder trees and smoky bays
if I find the code out of here
I'll walk the hills or swim the sea
drink ten Mai Tais on the beach
that'll crack open the head
and I'll ride that yolky brain bleed out
like a surfer on a golden wave
that's what I dream cross-legged
inside this burning white blazing
sun just within
and out of reach of everyone

Golden Hour

Fence mended and the wild cut back
I head down the alleyway and under
the magic archway through the shade
to bright blond sand and sirens going
fire trucks and aid cars cruising in
men climbing into wetsuits
fire boat fast cutting into the cove
all play in the vicinity stopped
as I look around and see cops
talking to a man and a woman
and two kids knee-deep in water
pointing I think to one out there
drifting just below the surface
the fire boat circling as divers wade in
like creatures from the black lagoon
monstrous I imagine they might appear
in those last four to seven minutes
the lungs full and heavy weighted
no longer seeking air but wide eye
sight clear as the soul chooses to go
either this way toward bubbling seal men
and the violence on shore or that way
toward light glory rays coming down
and the warm vast sky over all
so I ask which would you choose
with no guarantee as the dark
talons of evening cut across the sun

Fast Awake

I'm reaching for the amethyst
center of the sea
trying to name every tree
on the peninsula
but in the back of my mind
I'm worried about money
and calculating if I don't eat
I can save enough for school
how many pounds must I shed
to clear the hunger cobwebs
the dog scratching at the door
with that deep-woods look
room consumed by drinking rounds
crows loading up in the trees
and I am back in a brackish current
between falling apple puffs of smoke
so I ripple my way and sometimes
come up for air
sometimes eat the earth
eyes wide like meteors
burning in a green bay

Fugitive

The angry woman's house is a skull
listen to those orders what a bark
like a camp counselor on a field trip
I survived as a crow
the smartest crow on the block
from a headache this earthquake is born
you still with me on this one
it could go many ways
the funhouse of your star glasses
a ferry ride to the pineal gland
the grand foyer and the hot sun
with a tray of iced tea for the skeletons
a book of dismay
a cruise ship to paradise
and a spotlight on your soul
I know a place where we can hide out
a couple of lifetimes
nothing but umbrellas and sea waves
and no time reclining in the wind
with a hut to meditate in

Thank the Wind Alive

I tell stories to nothing but the walls
        photographs floating away
the old ones said three's a crowd
        and I got used to thinking that way
bewildered and climbing onto the bus
        heading into serious enemy territory

it's tough to mythologize basement pipes
        silent gym class at the end of the day
        and the afternoon gauntlet
        the dirt yards
        the railroad tracks

but home safe at last
        I'm with the best gods I know
coming through the television set

Zen Painting

The land goes on forever
       you might say
with a blue sliver river line
       and green-face rock crops
sun devils and heat devils
       and anvil cloud updrafts
hawk on a thermal riding away

no trail no road no town
       just pinyon spike and feral eyes
chittering chipmunks and stick snakes
       dry lightning in the hills
clouds coming in with storms
       and big boom of thunder

we only pass through

Diamond

At the breath's edge
　　　spirit leaves the body
to commune with exploding
　　　thought light arriving
opening eyes in the universe

black-winged agents placed
　　　a diamond in my head
to carry back into the world

I began full of force and fury
　　　among passionate creators
roaring in their ocean-making

but ink is a fuse in a burning door
　　　and each word etches away
what the diamond has to say

Thought Experiment

I'm painting the door to the garden
and reading *Orizaba Blues*
beneath the Buddha fountain
tending a stomach ulcer
and my tai chi den tien
glowing from the black
hole of several decisions
which means I am
in the basement
refining the invisible hand
reclining on waters of the deep
awake even when I sleep

Paralysis

What's out there becomes
too monstrous to name
clouds bunch up and lightning flares
food becomes an issue
I've got windows north and south
west through which I see the Sound
a fortress wall to guard the garden
here behind the iron gate

sawblade whine and hammer strike
reptilian shudder in grocery lines
cacophony and home delivery
the street is loaded with darkness
retreat to the castle and light a fire
cook whatever's left in the fridge

Slipping Through the Zones

I make my way through security
by having nothing at all
so X-ray me to the codes
even those are forgeries

hide behind pillars of guanine
you can't see among the caravans
young Adens tricking us into chains
thinking I'll go here and I'll go there
leaves chattering about lottery numbers
as wind blows them down the street

Miescher has declared this a no fly zone
with Frank and James it doesn't take
a Holmes to unlock this crick in the neck
and the radiant fury dying to be born

so I cruise the ergodic outposts
where a congregation of vapors sigh
and against all likelihood and odds
come to lay gifts at the infant feet
in a story of triumph disguised as defeat

Sabbatical Under the Bridge

I was once of that heroic voice
bringing heaven to the stones
the beach trembled underfoot
and every step I took
an artifact rattled to the surface
here an arrowhead
there a scraper of hides
and squinting in afternoon light
I saw the tanning racks
and the summer lean-tos
and by a code in the blood
I knew that silver moment
in the cool steel cut of wind
signaling the time
to go back over the hills
to winter homes on the river

Penrose Staircase

How can I be here and somewhere else
      how is a particle a wave
I work timber into place shoulder to the porch
I've thought through every move for days
      measured and cut measured and cut
and still it comes out different than I imagined

no design is exact yet I believe in the math of it
      but the more I go in the human world
      the farther off the angles seem
and though mathematically impossible
      two parallel lines do in fact meet
at the door to the house of my dreams

Island Time

Siren Song

a ferry ride from there to here
spikes of whitecaps on the sea
we slide up parallel to the island
so close you could almost touch it
and I imagine jumping over rail
a needle in the ice cold sound
a dream body striking west
and rising from the sunlit surf
blazing with desire and making it

on the island we find the trail
and hike up out of the creek bed
up and over the green slopes
trail mucked up from heavy rains
and throw ourselves step by step
into stinging nettles and spider webs
on powerful legs fueled by pollen
with the goat path switching back
through thistle banks to the bluff

here shed the weight of all worry
the lifetimes of shadow scenes
as evening settles on the cliffs
that shudder from incoming tides
with trees beaten back by storms
and the relentless blast of the straight
bull kelp drifting in the cove below
bell buoys ringing this way this way
in the singing wind and waves

New Arrival

He comes to the island with big dream
eyes burning all that's possible
walking the highway from Penn Cove
to Langley as dogs pick up on his scent
and he's collecting talking stones
mental notes from muscles he plucks
from the floating docks in Saratoga Bay
as heron armadas descend on the inlet
the moon shining over the mud flats
and good homes on the hill beaming
warmth fortune family and friends
a holiday you can actually believe
as he pushes through the window glow
and wills himself by force back in

The Bog

You gotta watch out
when you cross the bog
if you stop you're gonna sink in
lose a boot or worse
men coming down from the bar to smoke
have gone missing only to turn up
with a hand sticking out of the sand
or a foot poking out of a cliff wall
bog men bobbing around in liquid
underground spark of stone against stone
as the gel flesh rolls fluid and slow
through the black arms of sediment
so keep moving and step light
and fill your lungs with air

Double Bluff

White driftwood is a sand-blasted Egypt
and tidelines the new city blueprint
based on angular music and anxiety
here in the first knife-blade breeze
arriving at the leading edge of storm
with froth clouds and lightning flare
snake shadows sliding over the sound
and cabin smoke dark rising in the forest

yet the hawk above knows higher
and farther away you'll also see
men pulling crab pots out of the shallows
at dusk and their voices riding the air
as they drink to another day of good luck
saying why would you ever leave

On Entering

The question is
what is that woman looking at
as she stands there
next to the town sign
umbrella in her hand
motionless and wide-eyed

the men are out there
working on the power line
the white church hovers
in the green field

the house is a burned husk
with a shadow in the attic
overlooking the cove under
clouds flowing white and gray

Catch and Release

He waves and smiles and says
you guys look like celebrities
black jacket and blond hair
and wow now in this light
he's off ranting with spit froth
I got two springs in a row coming
one a high water point in the Rockies
four thousand fourteen feet above sea level
and now here since it's Thursday right
today's Thursday isn't it because
the restaurants are giving out free lunch
and man do they know how to spice it
I've got a Master's degree in Australia
my mark in the courtyards of Amsterdam
yoga lawyers bookstores bars
gray cut-outs in windows like it's 1873
as if time is always so you never die
but every five years they open a grave
and then they put another body in
can you imagine churning up the dead
and what that does to your mind I mean
everything is until you think about it

Winterfalling

What has to happen to a person
to say love is pathology
here in the Clyde Theater
as the old dramas play out
she loved him and him
got pregnant by him
but married him
and so now runs into him
which pisses him off
neighbors in the same row
expert on nails and paint
and seasons that slip away
with Friday matinees suspended
until next November
so it's just us again
and the street so quiet
you'd think the town was
abandoned and all these
faces in the windows ghosts

The Kiss of Life

You see
when you wake up and can't remember
if you cleared out the flower beds
or swept up the walkways
or repaired the sage garden arrow pond
and black stone twin-fish fountain
sky breaking open behind a white cloud
she says that shell is the horsehead
incoming wind raven stealing the sun
while on main street I'm peddling booklets
and saying maybe this will cure
the madman and his distortion box
red waves in his eyes when he claims
the mayor's wife is running the frog club
down the stone stairs in a secret grotto
where silence bounces back transformed
by cave crystals green as cat's eyes
a woman dancing in slow moonlight
with a blue star globe in her hands
like a glittering thought in the void
so put up another chalkboard mark
for this one good kiss today

The Doghouse

You've got no image
but you've got the gray
rain against the windows
you've got the old crowd
with absinthe laughter
and good old-fashioned
whiskey stares
and you've got the woman
climbing into bed who says
please no more nightmares

Dream Theater

What a sad tawdry place
for a final viewing
with faded red
curtains along the wall
broken or slumping seats
memories stuck in re-run

The Star

you see I'm trying to get
away from the booze hound
in the Mexican cantina
under these festive chili lights
like it was Christmas in July
like a heat spell that foretells
the end of the world
and launching off the planet
with a tear in the eye
and a hopeful woman floating
in her silver zero gravity suit
and that star just a number
where our great great grand
children will begin again
life with the same mix of
tragedy and loneliness and vice
and occasional tenderness
and a glass of green fantasy
but even here they come up
with those faces of broken
blood vessels like sculptures
rough-hewn from a raw scream
saying I left my distortion box
out there in the rain and now
it's picking up signals from old
Soviet Union cold war days
prairie wind and mile on mile of
empty road rolling right back
where the needle goes in
and the nurse explains this may
make you a little dizzy
and she's right and what a glorious
sea it is and that rickety dock
I dive from into liquid sky

to swim out through the sun's eye
into clouds of unknowing where
I see the great architecture of
crystalline light bridges I realize
are really only hanging cobwebs
as I look through a manhole cover
in the city of the dead trembling
breathless as I'm sucked back
into Langley by the sea
island spirit floating
in the never never mist
where when the desperate reach
that point of exhaustion
the last of the fuel burned
lights gone out and the final
relative buried in the common grave
I'm out here taking nothing
but what fits in these pockets
with the screen door open
and wind like a ghost rushing in
walking out through empty streets
and every step I feel like now
I've made it now I'll start again
until wait a minute wait a minute
as those steps circle back to town
over and over with less
to return to but the Bulldog
over the bay with the last
fishing boat beached and listing
dry on the sand with armies of
crabs none too happy with the way
their water's clouded up
marching up over the pylons
growing bigger as they come
their claws flashing like swords
as they descend on the homes
and click cut pluck up
sleeping people and snap

timbers in apocalyptic devastation
ha   that's one
to wake up from in a daze
saying what a doozy
to an empty room on a gray day
dressing slowly as a good citizen
filling a lunch box with an apple
and a sandwich wrapped in wax paper
then heading up the old road
under the mill smoke piling up
with tin hat crane operators
and massive movement of earth
as I pass the gate and stand among
the red spirits of the yawning
excavation pit while the whole
scene vanishes with a voice narrating
weather trends and ship lanes
and drinking songs and memories
old lays and things thought gone
you'd never believe were true
but making it up as we go along

Talking to Myself

Walk it off
walk it off

I'm here
to either slum it
in my fantasies
or project
past my death

and cold enough
to stay awake

The Myth

I want the great age
the ring of colossal construction
monuments that amaze
even seen from space
mighty works that vibrate
through generations and live

I'm standing on an empty road
the only word for it is wasteland
war couldn't cause this devastation
ground leveled peaks gone
no water no wind
time running out

we're sifting through ruins
with new reading skills
and others less attuned might
call this rock marsh or bog
until we find the cathedral
vine-covered steps and at last
the altar used for the sacrifice

two lights shine across a field
unwavering and clear as I go
and I seem to be getting nearer
though it takes forever to get there
on sluggish mud-sinking feet
but then I find myself
looking through another face
and leaning into a mysterious kiss

Off-Season Travelers

What a luxurious bed
   and through that window
      the sea
      seagulls
      an eagle at one point
         white tail feathers flashing
      in the light
         breaking through clouds
and what a scene
      as the tide surges in
         seals barking on the rocks
      and the tulips
         in the painting over the fireplace
      glowing like an X-ray
the walls burning
      then falling away

Eat Stone and Go On

He talks that old guy in the bar
and says I'm just trying to tell her
you know how those words and that tone
that sound that comes in like robbery
with clubs and knives or a documentary
the world has ways to shoot you down
and authorities are not arriving to help
it blurs in the explaining
but now I hope for shelter at least
and not to be hit by side flak

and the sweet dark empty street
when we finally push home
under the halo glow of the moon
and lie down in the intersection
yelling Take me now Take me now
then chuckle and rise and wander off
as winds breathe up the sandstone cliffs
and hawks grip tree limbs in sway
no dock or destination as stars slide
overhead like yellow dragonfish eyes
the way a thought keeps going till
I wake with you asleep at my side

What Should I Say?

With a few moments left
what should I say
that it was all worth it
somehow that's not enough
that I see a great golden field
where the afflicted shed their ills
and blaze   true
but that's not enough
that I love you still
across these waves
yes even so

The Morphic Field Hotel

Rough-hewn logs embedded in the mud
shaker roof green-layered with moss
a deck o'erlooking the cove west
a blue slip of land cutting into the sea
and a deep dream buttery moon rising
with whitetail fire glowing on the waves
as ghosts wander in the bone mist
rubbing hands together by warm fires
stately bodies carrying ancient faces
looking out through warped windows
their names on yellow ledger pages
fluttering as air sweeps through
and sparks fly up from the chimney
then coil into men with bent backs
carving trails from the beach to the well
where frogs under surface in the pools
fill the air with their night warbles
and wind slides through Madrona trees
lifting limbs with first feelers of spring

stuck in a 1938 Brown University yearbook
find Frank Foster the smarmy student president
a cruel general and corporate henchman
tax-paying fire-builder in plaid jacket and flap hat
out at the water's edge fishing at dawn
not a sound from the world but an occasional loon
then ducks rising with the light
and here's Paul Welch we used to call Lantern Jaw
Forbes and Robert Reigler arrested on Bankers Row
and happy Marvin Carton known as The Maestro
Leonard Carpenter the lawyer of Buckingham
and many many more who went to war
scholars and athletes now caught in this book
stuck on a dust covered cabin shelf

with a dry ribbon Underwood typewriter
and a frontier fireplace glowing with heat

we float in this room
on a cliff over the sea
staring centuries
into the heart of fire
the equation for wind
and never-ending waves
in the light in the water
in our blood in our dreams

a couple went out one night for a walk
down along the beach and were caught
when the tide came surging back in
cutting them off and trapping them
against sandstone cliffs in the cove
and at first they tried to climb the rocks
but waves yanked them right back out
as they struggled to swim looking up
at the fire still flickering in the room

he came to the end of the world
looking out to sea with one intention
to kill the body or kill the self
so lined the floor with bottles and drank
lit a fire that burned hot and high
drew deep fueling wind into the room
through windows and the wide open door
filling the fireplace so the fire seethed
and a spark shot free and caught the rug
ember-burning as it slept and glowed
then crept like a spider up the wall
as the dry-grass curtains flared
the man trapped in the orange black
feathers of air-engorged flame
examining a page in an old yearbook
as if there he might find a familiar face

spectral people on the lawn
under gentle glowing constellations
dance and smoke in the white gazebo
and walk the trail down to the beach
and climb into boats and row out
into the cove and the rotating sky
flowing soul lights coming and going
one here with a hand on a doorknob
hotel hallways throbbing with laughter
river stone fireplace chugging away
guests in leather chairs reading books
as arriving night comes swirling down
with heavy earth-swallowing clouds
and rain and wind and nothing out there
but black night sight snuffed out
and the world shrunk down to a fist

and in this room the fireplace snaps
and lamp lights occasionally flicker
vicious and menacing ocean sounds rise
and sparks from the chimney float up
like soul rockets afterburning then gone
and the ghost hotel hoves in the middle
of spiral-punching whip-cracking winds
that slither through windows and doors
ruffling the framed film posters on the walls
of movie stars who swept in like magic
beings who lived among us and slept in
rooms thinking and dreaming and reading
titles on book spines in the upper alcove
gazing through windows by the back stove
and reaching with hands like this one
I extend to you from a yearbook
to type up letters on an Underwood relic
notes on hikes through the hill grass trails
among trees with those twisted shapes

and even stones lie flat on the ground
with wind from the straight flowing up
and scoring the clouds with a parting cut
as sun bolts appear that light the world
and shimmer over snakeskin roads
and pools and ponds where we dive in
disappearing under cold water depth
as silver threads fall from a sun coin above
and we rise and step out perfectly renewed
to walk the shore through Madrona trees
each an individual flame of eternity

and it takes eternity to read it all
as mind that writes the world keeps writing
and mind that reads the world keeps reading
and thoughts like that'll make a person
stop in mid-step and regard the horizon
seeing everything furiously happening
white mountain peaks dissolving in distance
back-diving through Big Dipper and Gemini
The Bear scrolling over us night into day
night into mysterious hill blossoms
with hotel windows glittering like diamonds
as I read the life of John Keats
at the moment he's hiking the chilly moors
in a storm like this one out of the north
talons of wind clawing the spring
as he reads every grove stone river and gull
a young man walking alive the green
magical rain-drenched landscape
soaked to the skin and in love with the cold
because he's on fire inside and stoked
with passion-thoughts of beauty
so that water steams from his shoulders
as he hikes and eventually finds
a little hotel overlooking the cove
where he climbs the grand stairs
and pushing through the door

enters a lobby with a desk and couch
and fox pelts on the walls
and leather chairs and big fire going
there in a river rock hearth
so he takes a room and sits at a table
lights a candle and begins to write

Ferry Run

We climb on board
and head to the bow
feel the wind
and stroke of clouds

we cross and stand
re-cross and sway
and reach for land
that slips away

About the Author

Douglas Cole has published five collections of poetry and a novella. His work has appeared in several anthologies and journals such as *The Chicago Quarterly Review, The Galway Review, Louisiana Literature, Two Thirds North, Mid-American Poetry Review, Red Rock Review,* and *Slipstream.* He has been nominated twice for a Pushcart and Best of the Net and has received both the Leslie Hunt Memorial Prize in Poetry and the Best of Poetry Award from *Clapboard House.* His website is douglastcole.com.

www.ingramcontent.com/pod-product-compliance
Lightning Source LLC
Chambersburg PA
CBHW030958090426
42737CB00007B/593